The Learning Book

The Learning Book

From the works of L. Ron Hubbard

Delphian Press

Compiled from the works of L. Ron Hubbard by the faculty of the Delphian School.

Published by Delphian Press, 20950 S.W. Rock Creek Road, Sheridan, OR 97378.

International Issue Authority granted 1983.

Senior Editor: Alan H. Larson
Editor: Dave Hendry
Illustrations: Anne Geiberger

ISBN 0-89739-004-0

We are deeply indebted to L. Ron Hubbard who has, through over
29 years of research, pioneered an extremely workable methodology
of study and education which has effectively opened the doors of
education to many tens of thousands. In presenting the most basic of
Mr. Hubbard's discoveries in a form easily understood by them, it is
our certainty that more and more students will discover for
themselves the joys of learning.

If you would like to do a course, at home, based on the contents of this
book, send $2.50 and your name and address to: The Learning Book
c/o The Delphian School, 20950 S.W. Rock Creek Road, Sheridan, OR
97378. You will receive a complete and easy-to-follow course outline.

Printed in U.S.A.

88 89 90 91 92 93 94 95   10 9 8 7 6 5 4 3 2

ANY TIME YOU READ
A WORD IN THIS BOOK
THAT YOU DO NOT
UNDERSTAND, LOOK IT
UP IN A DICTIONARY
OR THE GLOSSARY AT
THE BACK OF THIS BOOK.

To **study** is to look at something

to find out more about it.

There are many ways to study.

People study so they can know how to do things.

For someone to study, there has to be something there to study.

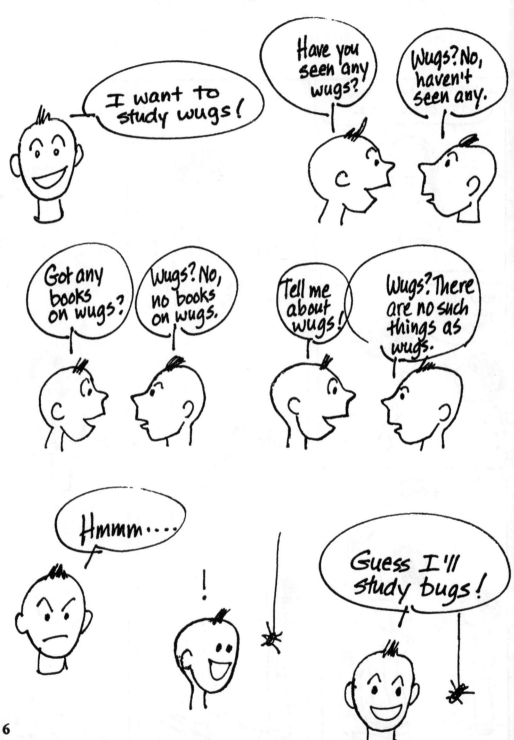

For you to study something, you must know there is something about it that you don't know.

Before you start studying something, find out if there is something you could learn about it.

How
to
study

1. Get the information.

2. See how you can use it.

3. Use it!

Studying is fun.

As you study you can speed along,
learning more and more and being
able to do more and more.

But sometimes
you run into the...

BARRIERS
TO
STUDY

A barrier is  like a wall.

It keeps you from
going somewhere.

When you hit one of the barriers
to study, you don't feel very good,
and you **don't** feel like studying
any more.

BUT...

You can go through
the barriers to study.

There are
3
barriers to
study.

And there are special ways to go through each one!

THE MOST IMPORTANT BARRIER:

THE MISUNDERSTOOD WORD

Suppose you had an idea...

and you found someone to tell about it and told him.

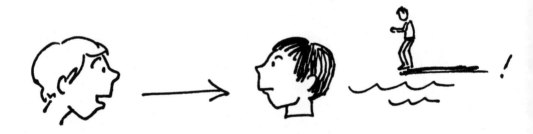

How would you tell him?

You use words, of course!

But—What if you tried to tell
him with words he didn't understand?

Neither of you would get much
swimming done.

It's the same thing with study.

As long as you know all the words, you can study and have a good time.

You can use what you are studying.

But if you didn't know all the words, you would have a hard time.

And you couldn't use what you had studied.

In the same way, if you had the wrong meaning for a word you read,

you could get some pretty strange ideas...

And you would not be able to
use what you had studied.

A
WORD
you hear or read
that you don't know
the meaning of, or
that you have the
wrong meaning for, is
called a...

MISUNDERSTOOD WORD

There are different ways that a word can be misunderstood.

You can have a totally wrong
meaning for a word.

You might make up a wrong
meaning, or someone might tell
you a meaning he made up.

You can have a meaning that is
not right, but is a little like the
right meaning.

You might not know enough about what a word means. If you knew an owl was a bird, but didn't know any more about owls, that would not be enough.

You can have a meaning that does
not fit the word the way it is used
in the sentence. (In the sentence above,
"dressing" really means "making
something ready to be cooked.")

You can have a meaning for a word that is really the meaning for a different word that sounds the same.

You can use one word in place of another word. This is a way that a word can be misunderstood, because the two words do not really mean the same thing.

You can be missing one of the
meanings of a word.

You might not have any
meaning for a word at all.

You may not want to know
what a word means.

The
MISUNDERSTOOD
WORD
(M.U. for short)
is a
barrier to study.

A **symbol** is a mark or a sign that means something.

Symbols can be misunderstood
in the same ways that words can
be misunderstood.

When you go past a
misunderstood word or symbol,
you feel blank, or washed-out —
you may yawn —

Then you may feel not there...

...and kind of nervous and upset.

If you go past a **lot** of m.u.'s, you may start to dislike what you are studying.

You might start complaining and blaming others.

You might even **leave!**

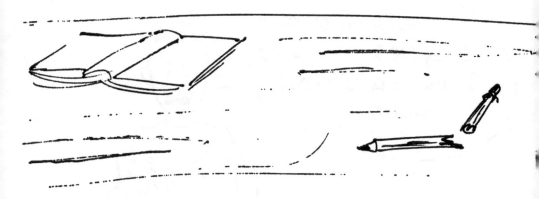

And not want to study that any more.

Or, if you had to keep studying,
you might just memorize the
information without really
learning anything.
You might get a good score on
a test…

…but not be able to **use** what
you had studied.

The special way to go through
the barrier of the misunderstood
word is:

FIND OUT
WHAT THE
WORD MEANS!

You start feeling bad **after** you pass the M.U.

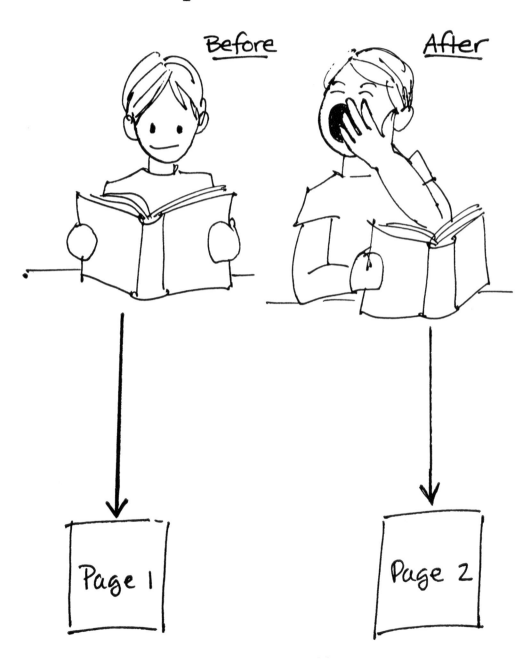

The M.U. is at the end of where you were not having trouble.

To find the M.U., go back to
where you were not having trouble...

then find out where you began
having trouble.

Look for the M.U. right at the end of where you were not having trouble.

Whenever you feel or do any of the things that happen when you pass an M.U., go back to where you were *not* having trouble and find the word or symbol you didn't understand.

SIMPLE
WORDS

You might think that it is
the BIG words which are most
misunderstood.

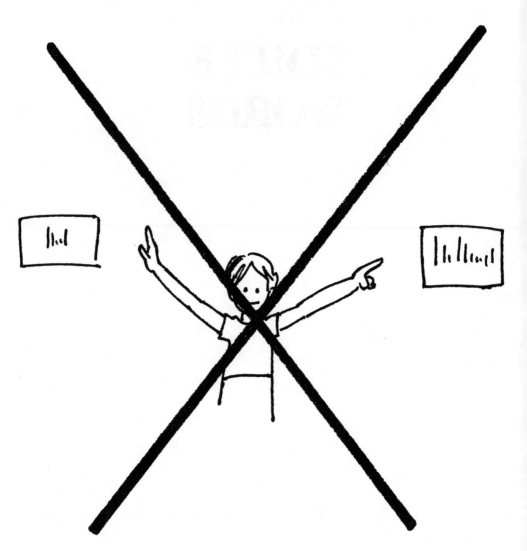

This is NOT true.

Simple words (like "a," "the," "or" and "an") are often misunderstood.

When you are looking for a misunderstood word, don't just look for big words. Look for simple words also.

LOOK RIGHT *BEFORE* YOU STARTED HAVING TROUBLE

LOOK FOR *SIMPLE* WORDS TOO

LOOKING
UP
WORDS

Learning the meaning of a word
is just like studying anything else.
You study it so that you can use it.

The way to learn the meaning of
a word is:

FIND IT IN THE
DICTIONARY.

Apple: A fruit
that is round
and red.

READ THE
MEANING.

AND...

USE IT!

The way to use and really understand a word is to make sentences using the word.

Use the word in sentences until you **really** understand it and can use it. (This could take ten or more sentences.)

Some words have more
than one meaning.

leg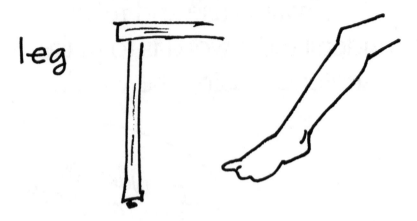

When you look up a word, you
must learn **all** the meanings. That
way, when you see the word used
a different way later, you will
understand it.

To look up a word that has more
than one meaning, **FIRST** find
and learn the meaning that fits
what you are studying. (If that
meaning isn't in your dictionary,
find a bigger dictionary.)

THEN learn the other meanings.

For each meaning of the word, use it in sentences until you **really** understand it. (Remember, this could take ten or more sentences.)

The word may have special
meanings that are not used every
day, or old meanings that are not
used any more. The dictionary
will say that they are special or
old meanings.

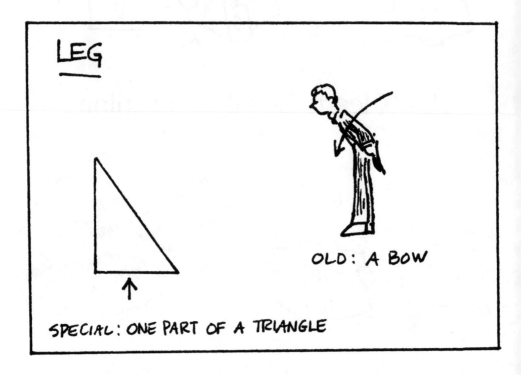

You do not need to learn a
special or old meaning of a word
unless it is the meaning that fits
what you are studying.

The dictionary may also tell
where the word first came from.
Be sure to learn this.

Learning where a word came
from will help you really
understand the word.

The dictionary may show a meaning for a group of words the word is used in. The group of words has a different meaning than the meanings of the words in it.

SHAKE A LEG
means to dance

Learn that too, the same way you learned the other meanings for the word.

The dictionary may say things like how to use the word with other words. It may show other words that have the same or almost the same meaning.

The boy had a <u>kitten</u>.
<u>Kittens</u> like to play.

<u>Kitty</u> also means kitten.

KITTEN

Learn anything else the dictionary tells about the word.

BUT—

What if there is a misunderstood word or symbol in what you are reading in the dictionary?

What should you do?

Look it up, too!

Learn it the same way you learn any word. Then go back to the word you started with.

After you have found out what the word means, you can start studying again.

Start at the place where the M.U. was, so you will be sure to understand everything you are studying.

ANOTHER BARRIER:
NOT HAVING MASS

The person on the page just before this one read, and read, and read, and read, and read, and read, and read, and read, and read, and read, and read, and read, and read.

He just kept on reading.

When you study about something, but you don't have the *mass* that goes with it (the thing itself or something that you can use in place of the thing) you can start to feel bad.

For example, if someone was telling you about cats, but you didn't have the **mass** of cats, you might feel squashed, or bent, or spinny, or sort of dead, or bored —

BUT —if you had the **mass** —a cat or something that you could pretend was a cat —you would feel fine, and enjoy learning about cats.

When you don't have the mass for what you are studying, you may feel like you're up against something...

but you can't move through it.

You may feel like this.

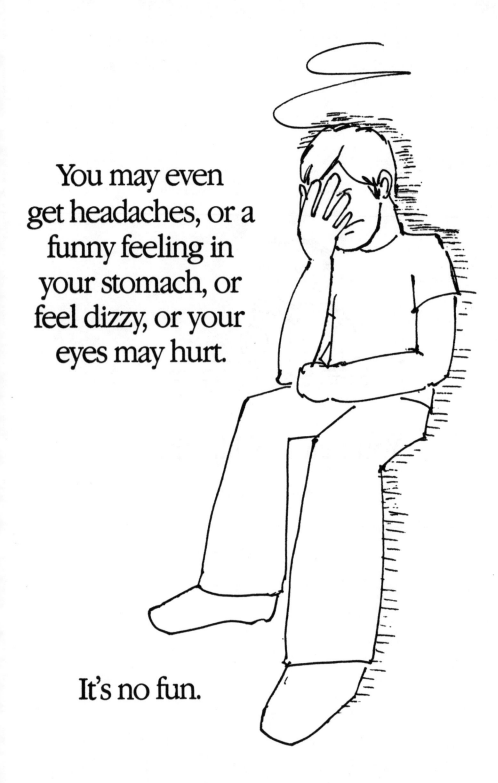

You may even
get headaches, or a
funny feeling in
your stomach, or
feel dizzy, or your
eyes may hurt.

It's no fun.

NOT HAVING THE *MASS* FOR WHAT YOU ARE STUDYING
is a barrier to study.

There are four special ways to go through this barrier. They are...

1. Look at the thing you are studying about. This is the best way.

2. Make a **CLAY DEMO**

("Demo" comes from the word "demonstration." It means showing how something is or works.)

The way to make a clay demo is to take a big glob of clay and shape it to show what you are studying about.

When you make a clay demo,
make a little sign, or label, for each
thing you shape out of the clay.

When you're done, make a label
for the whole thing.

In a clay demo, the **clay** must
show the thing you are
demonstrating. Someone else
should be able to look at your
clay demo and tell what idea it is

demonstrating without you
telling him what it is about.

3. Get a bunch of things and use them to show what you are studying about.

This is called demoing, and the things you use are called a demo kit.

4. Make or find a picture of what you are studying.

Any time you demonstrate, REALLY *SHOW* THE THING.

That way you get the *mass*.

If you always make sure to have the mass for what you are studying, you will never run into this barrier. Wouldn't that be nice?

ANOTHER BARRIER:

THE SKIPPED GRADIENT

What if when you were little, you had just learned to ride a tricycle, and someone handed you some **car** keys and asked you to drive to the store?

Even if you could get in the car and start the motor, you would still feel pretty mixed up.

Trying to drive a car after you had
just learned to ride a tricycle
would be something like trying
to get to the top of a very high cliff

from the very bottom.

One way to get up
the cliff would be
to build steps going
up it, and
then

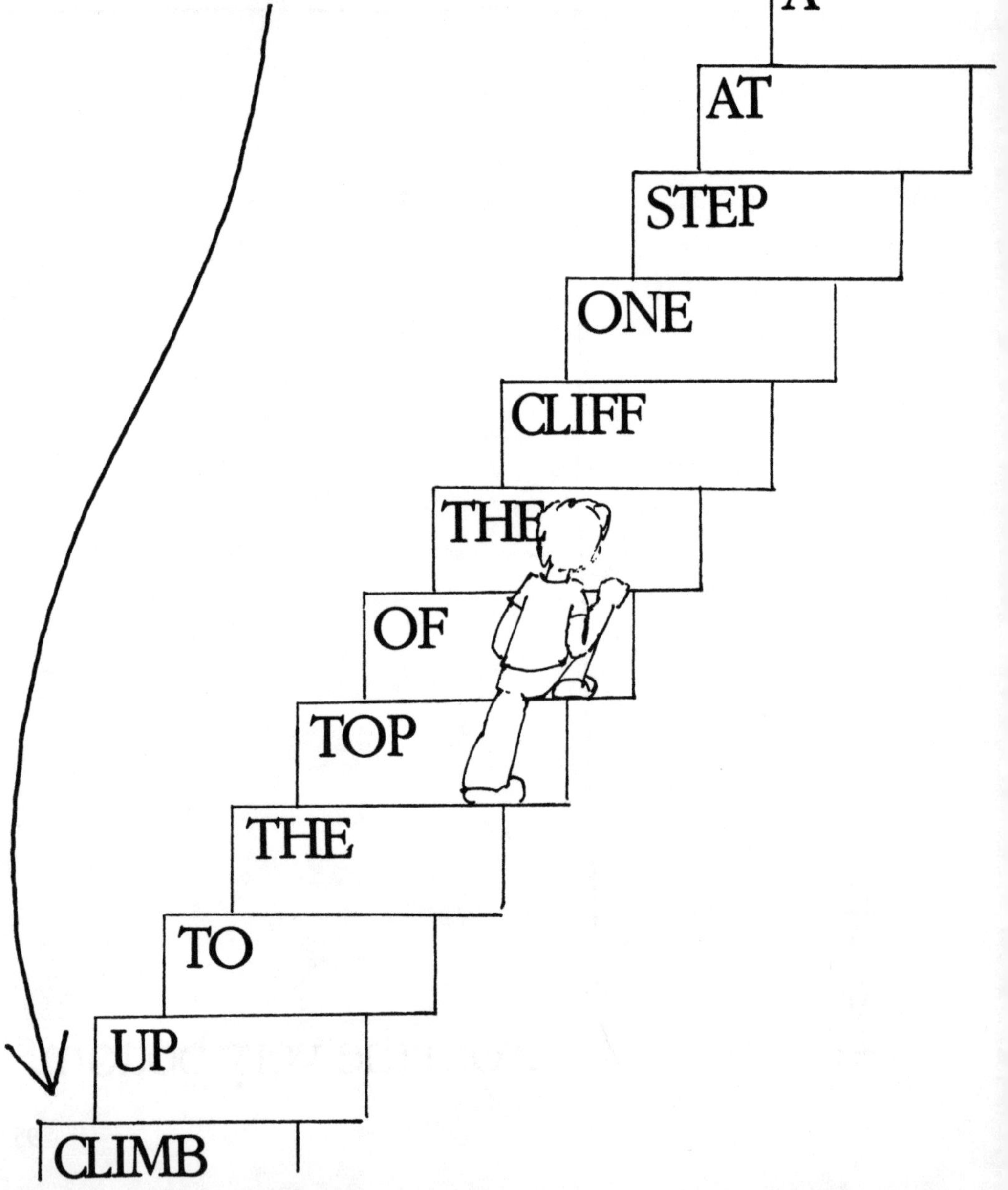

TIME.

A

AT

STEP

ONE

CLIFF

THE

OF

TOP

THE

TO

UP

CLIMB

Something that moves up one step at a time is called a gradient. The way to learn something is to study it on a gradient, one step up at a time.

THAT WAY,
YOU GET
TO THE TOP!

When you study something on a gradient, each step has a bit more to it than the one before.

Each time you finish a step, you can do more.

What if, while you were climbing the steps up to the top of the cliff, you couldn't seem to get up the next step?

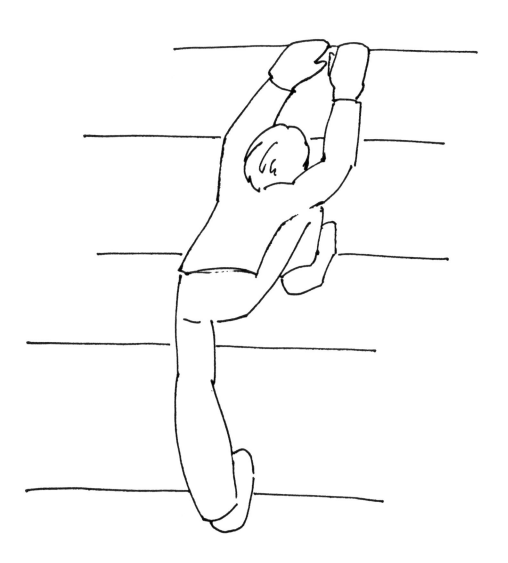

YOU MUST HAVE MISSED A STEP

Look back, find
the step you
missed,

and climb it.

Then the next step is easy.

When you are studying, if you skip one
of the steps, or don't learn one
of the steps all the way, you have

skipped a gradient.

Then you feel confused, or mixed up.

Usually skipped gradients
happen when you are learning
how to **do** things.

The SKIPPED GRADIENT is a barrier to study.

Remember that the reason you feel confused about a step you are on is because you didn't get one **BEFORE,** not because the one you are on is too hard.

The special way to get through this barrier is to go back to the step you were on **BEFORE** you started feeling confused and go over that one until you know it all the way.

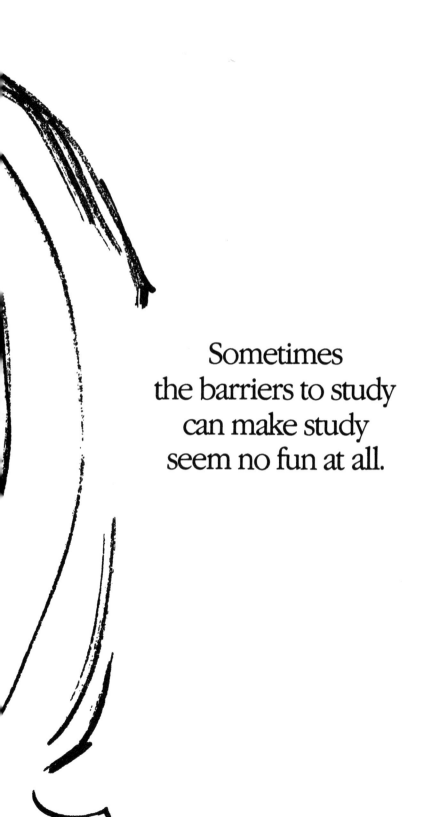

Sometimes
the barriers to study
can make study
seem no fun at all.

BUT NOW YOU KNOW HOW TO STUDY.

Look up misunderstood words.

Look at or demo what you're studying about.

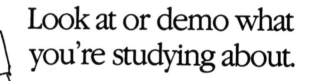

Go one step at a time.

YOU KNOW WHAT THE BARRIERS TO STUDY ARE, AND YOU KNOW THE SPECIAL WAYS THROUGH.

Feel blank?

or sleepy?

or like you don't want to study any more?

Feel washed-out?

 or not there?

or sort of nervous and upset?

Do you dislike what you're studying?

Are you complaining and blaming others?

Can't you **use** what you studied?

Find the word you didn't understand

and look it up!

 Feel squashed?

or bored?

 or like you're not
getting anywhere?

 Feel bent?

or spinny or dizzy?

 or sort of dead?

Getting headaches
or a funny feeling
in your stomach?

Do your eyes hurt?

Do you feel like this?

Look at or demo

[CAT]

the thing you're studying about.

FEEL CONFUSED?

Go back to where you were last doing well, and do *that* until you've really got it.

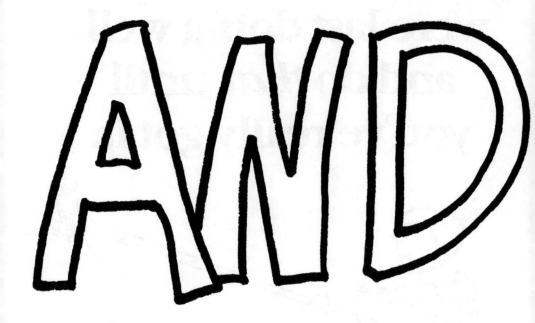

HAVE FUN

LEARNING LOTS OF
NEW THINGS!

GLOSSARY

Here are some of the words used
in this book and the meanings which
fit the way the words are used.

barrier

anything that stops things
or people.

bent

crooked; twisted; curved.

blank

having nothing there; empty.

bored

not interested in what you're doing and tired of doing it.

clay demo

a way of demonstrating what you are studying by using clay.

demo

short for "demonstration" or "demonstrate."

demo kit

a bunch of small things kept in a box, can or bag. The things are used to demonstrate what you are studying.

demonstrate

show the way something is or
how something works.

demonstration

showing the way something is or
how something works.

dizzy

light-headed; feeling like you are spinning around and as if you might fall.

glossary

a list of some of the words used
in a book and the meanings which
fit the way those words are used.

gradient

something that moves up one
step at a time.

idea

something you think; thought.

important

having a lot of value.

My baby brother is very important to me.

information

things you can learn and know.

learning

finding out about something, or
finding out how to do something
and being able to do it.

mass

a quantity of matter.

matter

what things are made of.

misunderstood

1. not understood; understood incorrectly.

2. a word that is not understood or is understood incorrectly.

MU

short for "misunderstood."

nervous

feeling kind of shaky and uneasy; jumpy; worried.

purpose

something you are trying to get done; the reason for doing something.

skipped

missed; not done; left out.

spinny

feeling as if you are turning around and around; dizzy.

squashed

pressed flat; squeezed; mashed.

study

look at something to find out more about it.

studying

looking at something to find out more about it.

symbol

a mark or a sign that means something.

Equals!

understand

know fully; have a clear and true idea of.

understood

fully known.

washed-out

very tired and weak.

word

letters or sounds put together that mean something.